POPULAR DELUSIONS

SANCTIONED BY

THE CHURCH OF ENGLAND.

An Essay.

BY

WILLIAM STOKES.

"*Prove all things; hold fast that which is good.*"—1 Thessalonians v. 21.

LONDON:

ELLIOTT STOCK, 62, PATERNOSTER ROW.

1876.

POPULAR DELUSIONS

SANCTIONED BY

THE CHURCH OF ENGLAND.

An Essay.

BY

WILLIAM STOKES.

"*Prove all things; hold fast that which is good.*" —1 Thessalonians v. 21.

LONDON:

ELLIOTT STOCK, 62, PATERNOSTER ROW.

1876.

PREFACE.

The Author of the following Essay desires that his object should be understood. His aim is to draw the attention of his Fellow-Christians to what he believes to be grievous Errors, which impede the progress of true Religion. The Delusions, which he thinks he has clearly proved to be sanctioned by the Church of England, are also sanctioned by other State-established Churches; and it is likely these Errors may be traced to the general neglect of the Apostolic doctrine, that "*The weapons of our warfare are not carnal, but mighty through God to the pulling down of strongholds.*" (2 Corinthians x. 4.) Teachers and Preachers under the Christian Dispensation have no *temporal* power, their power being only that of persuasion in the preaching of the Gospel; and this strictly agrees with the declaration of our Lord:—"*My kingdom is not of this world: if my kingdom were of this world, then would my servants fight, that I should not be delivered to the Jews: but now is my kingdom not from hence.*" (John xviii. 36.)

Rochdale; May, 1876.

CONTENTS.

CHAPTER I.

CHAPTER II.

CHAPTER III.

APPENDIX.

POPULAR DELUSIONS,

&c.

CHAPTER I.

INTRODUCTORY.

Fundamental Principle: The Supremacy of Holy Scripture

"*To the law and to the testimony: if they speak not according to this word, it is because there is no light in them.*" Isaiah, viii. 20.

It is an unspeakable advantage, on all disputed questions, when the rival disputants have within their reach, some common ground of appeal, or some acknowledged authority to which they may refer their clashing opinions, and to whose decision they are mutually pledged to submit. It goes far to prevent mere logomachies, and to hold in check those impulsive combatants who are always more ready to dogmatise than to reason, and more disposed to indulge in a useless verbosity than to exercise diligence in the honest pursuit of important truth. And this appeal does even more than this, for if the tribunal be a final one, which, in the case of Holy Scripture, it will ever be, it must, in all candour and common fairness, terminate the dispute, and close the controversy. But where no such authority exists, and no such an appeal can be made, the contending disputants degenerate into empty wranglers, who, in Miltonic phrase,

"Find no end in wandering mazes lost."

In the present instance we possess this great advantage—having Holy Scripture as the final judge, and the ultimate appeal, on whatever controverted points may arise during the discussion. And it increases this advantage when it is remembered that this sacred authority is mutually acknowledged, and that the fundamental principle is already accepted by all the parties concerned. Consequently, it will be taking no undue liberty with the Church of England to demand of that church, with its numerous officials, that it should be bound by its own declarations, and that its singular pretensions should be rigidly subjected to the test, which the whole of its members profess to revere. This test is not created or assumed for the occasion, but has been for centuries the avowed belief of the Church of England, as the following selections from its own articles will abundantly prove:—

In *Article 6th*, it is distinctly stated that "Holy Scripture containeth all things necessary to salvation, so that whatever is not read therein, nor may be proved thereby, is not to be required of any man, that it should be believed as an article of the Faith, or be thought requisite or necessary to salvation."

Article the 17th closes with the following sentence:—"——— and in our doings, that Will of God is to be followed, which we have expressly declared unto us in the Word of God."

Article 20th, after claiming for the Church power to "decree Rites or Ceremonies, and authority in Controversies of Faith," adds this significant caution—"And yet it is not lawful for the Church to ordain anything that is contrary to God's Word written, neither may it so expound one place of Scripture that it be repugnant to another." These words clearly imply that "God's Word written," is, or ought to be, the supreme law of the Church.

Article 21st, which treats of the authority of "General Councils," very properly limits the action of those formidable bodies, by the higher authority of the Word of God, and boldly affirms that "things ordained by them as necessary to salvation have neither strength nor authority, unless it may be declared that they be taken out of holy Scripture."

Article 34th, "Of the Traditions of the Church," teaches the same doctrine when it asserts that those traditions "may be changed according to the diversities of countries, times, and men's manners, so that nothing be ordained against God's Word," and it recommends an open rebuke for such disobedient persons as "break the traditions and ceremonies of the Church, *which be not repugnant to the Word of God.*"

These extracts show conclusively that the Church of England acknowledges the supremacy of Holy Scripture, and as a consequence must, on the score of a common consistency, bow to that authority as a tribunal from which there can be no appeal. Its whole ritual and claims, its pretensions to superiority over other sects and religious bodies, with its various ceremonies of every kind, must be at once and for ever rigidly subjected to this supreme test. If they accord with the Word of God, they can suffer nothing from the severest investigation, but will appear all the brighter—all the more divine—in proportion to the closeness of the examination. But if they are not authentic or divine—if they have sprung out of the corruptions of "the dark ages," which for centuries gave both law and religion to a slumbering Europe, and are but human inventions after all—the sooner this is laid bare to the whole world, the sooner will ecclesiastical pretences, that foster pride, and are doing so much to "sow discord among brethren," fall mutilated and helpless, like the ancient Dagon before the Divine Ark.

The object of the following treatise is to test these pretensions by Holy Scripture, and, if possible, to determine once for all whether they are of divine or of but human origin, and whether they are essential to the authority, the dignity, or the solid usefulness of a Christian church. The great importance of the examination may be gathered from a variety of sources, such as the conduct of the Bereans in the purest age of the Church, and the opinions of celebrated men whom the suffrages of successive generations have admitted to the highest honours among their compeers.

The Apostle of the Gentiles, with Silas, his fellow-traveller, were sent away by night from Thessalonica to Berea, where, as usual, they went into the synagogue of the Jews. The Bereans "were more noble than those of Thessalonica, in that they received the word with all readiness of mind, and *searched the Scriptures daily*, whether those things were so." This noble testimony to the manly conduct of the Bereans is all the more valuable on two accounts; first, it is an *inspired* testimony, expressive of the Divine approbation; and, secondly, the test of Holy Scripture was applied to the doctrine of an inspired apostle, who, by virtue of office, was one of the highest dignitaries the Church of God has ever had. And if the test was so applied to an apostolic man, with the avowed approval of the Most High himself, can it be wrong to apply it to humbler officials, such as popes, cardinals, archbishops, bishops, deans, rectors, vicars, and all other persons, who lay claim to distinction in the Church of God? Where an inspired apostle submitted to the ordeal, surely men in a less elevated position have no right to complain when placed on the same level with a mighty Paul! The limited space allotted to this publication will confine the writer to a bare selection of other authorities in favour of the fundamental principle already asserted, but the following will be amply sufficient for the purpose.

The Prince of British poets, John Milton, affirms this principle with characteristic distinctness and power. He says, "True religion is the true worship and service of God, learned and believed from the Word of God only. No man or angel can know how God would be worshipped and served unless God reveal it; he hath revealed and taught it us in the Holy Scriptures by inspired ministers, and in the gospel by his own Son and his apostles, with strictest command to reject all other traditions or additions whatsoever. . . . With good and religious reason, therefore, all Protestant churches, with one consent, maintain these two points, as the main principles of true religion, that the rule of true religion is the word of God only, and that their faith ought not to be an implicit faith, that is, to believe, though as the church believes, against or without express authority of Scripture."*

That distinguished divine and ornament of the Church of England, William Chillingworth, in one of the finest passages ever penned, expresses himself on this great doctrine thus: "I, for my part, after a long and (as I verily believe and hope) impartial search of the true way to eternal happiness, do profess plainly that I cannot find any rest for the sole of my foot but upon this rock only. I see plainly, and with my own eyes, that there are popes against popes, councils against councils, some fathers against others, the same fathers against themselves, a consent of fathers of one age against a consent of fathers of another age, the church of one age against the church of another age; in a word, there is no sufficient certainty but of Scripture only for any considering man to build upon." After some similar remarks, he adds, in a strain of noble confidence in divine truth, "Propose me anything out of this book [the Bible], and require whether I believe or no, and, seem it never so incomprehensible to human reason, I will subscribe it with hand and heart, as knowing no demonstration can be stronger than this—God hath said so, therefore it is true."†

John Locke, one of the most profound thinkers England ever had, maintains the same fundamental principle in his great work on the *Human Understanding*, in these expressive and conclusive terms: "Whatever God hath revealed

* Prose Works, Vol. ii., pp. 209, 210.

† 'Religion of Protestants: a Safe Way,' &c.. 6th chapter.

is certainly true ; no doubt can be made of it. This is the proper object of faith. Whatsoever is divine revelation ought to overrule all our opinions, prejudices, and interests. and hath a right to be received with a full assent."*

To these influential authorities numerous additions could easily be made were they required ; but this is not needed, since it is obvious to every thoughful and impartial person that the Holy Scriptures are supreme over all rites, ceremonies, and practices of an ecclesiastical character, and that no professed church can be a true church of God that does not bow to His revealed will as its highest law.

The beautiful encomium on the Bible, written by that eminent Orientalist, Sir William Jones, will be a fitting close to this introductory chapter, and will prove that the foregoing testimonies to the supremacy of the Word of God are not the inflated exaggerations of emotional partizans, but that they grow out of the eternal truth ; that while "all flesh is as grass," yet "the word of the Lord endureth for ever." His eloquent words are these :—

"I have carefully and regularly perused these Holy Scriptures, and I am of opinion that this volume, independently of its divine origin, contains more true sublimity, more exquisite beauty, more pure morality, more important history, and finer strains both of poetry and eloquence, than can be collected from all other books, in whatever age or language they may have been written."†

* *The Human Understanding.* Book 4. chap. 18. p. 352.

† Found written in his Bible. He died at the premature age of 48.

CHAPTER II.

Consecration.

Consecration, according to Dr. Eadie, "is the devoting or setting apart of any persons, things, or places to the worship and service of God. Churches, churchyards, the sacred vessels, and other utensils belonging to the worship of God, are consecrated things; but the Church of Rome consecrates almost everything, as bells, candles, water, oil, crosses, pictures, &c., beside churches, chapels, monasteries, and other religious houses."*

During the impeachment of Archbishop Laud in 1643-45, that prelate employed an expression that may be regarded as the clerical meaning to be attached to the otherwise mysterious rite of consecration. Having been charged with a "superstitious manner of consecrating chapels, churches, and churchyards," he replied, "*If churches were not consecrated, they would not be holy;*" and the natural inference is, that he would say precisely the same thing of churchyards, whence it would follow that the "consecration" of a common burying-ground, if but attached to a church, makes it "holy" too.†

Very similar is the practical view taken of the succeeding rite of "confirmation," as the following common-place announcement will clearly show. On the cover of "St.

* Eadie's 'Ecclesiastical Cyclopædia.' *In loco.*

† Neal's 'History of the Puritans,' vol. ii., p. 304.

Chad's (Rochdale) Parish Magazine for January, 1876," there appeared this official statement for the instruction of the parishioners :—" For the information of our readers, we may briefly state that Confirmation is a holy ordinance, used from the time of the apostles, in which, through the laying on of the bishop's hands with prayer, the baptized receive the gifts of the Holy Spirit ;" and it proceeds to declare, "then they are confirmed or strengthened (for that is the meaning of the word confirmed) by fresh grace from heaven, given to them by Christ, through His servant the bishop." This is not the place for demanding *scriptural* proof of these extraordinary assumptions, that being reserved for a thorough scrutiny hereafter ; it is therefore enough to say of this too ordinary statement, at present, that no part whatever of Holy Scripture favours these exorbitant pretensions in the remotest possible degree.

But " Consecration " must carry some other meaning than that of making holy persons and things with which it is brought into contact, or what can be made of the case of Charles the Bald, grandson of Charlemagne, as given by Hallam, the historian, in these words :—" No one," says that dethroned ruler, " ought to have degraded me from the throne *to which I was consecrated*, until at least I had been heard and judged by the bishops, *through whose ministry I was consecrated*, who are called the thrones of God, in which God sitteth, and by whom He dispenses His judgments ; to whose paternal chastisement I was willing to submit, and do still submit myself."*

If, according to Archbishop Laud, the act of consecration makes things and persons alike holy, may it not be asked

* 'Middle Ages,' chap. 7, p. 417.

in reference to the above unfortunate ruler, "What was made holy, the man or the throne, or both?" Priestly hands performed the ceremony whatever it may have been; did they, "who are called the thrones of God," also impart "the gifts of the Holy Spirit," as claimed for the Rochdale Confirmation, and so "set apart" both the king and the throne for some holy purpose to which other rulers and their thrones could present no claim? Or is consecration, after all, but a fallacy, or an empty pretence? Is it a divine institution, or but a priestly invention for the delusion of mankind? As this subject will require an extended investigation, it may aid the general enquiry to consider "Consecration" in reference to buildings, persons, churchyards, flags, banners, war vessels, and war material of all other kinds. This course will bring to light the origin, the delusiveness and utter futility of the much vaunted consecration of the Church of England.

§ I.—The Consecration of Buildings.

Is it necessary to *consecrate* a building of any kind? Is there any divine command to that effect? If so, where is it to be found? In what part of Holy Scripture? And *can* the act of consecration, by any possibility whatever, make a building "holy?"

To determine these different points, it will be useful, if not absolutely necessary, to review so much of the history and consecration of churches as will penetrate or remove the obscurity that has been so long allowed to hover over the general question of consecrated places. That there were none whatever in the apostolic age is evident beyond all doubt, and no competent authority has ever attempted to prove the contrary. That sacred place, the "upper room," where the Saviour and his disciples kept the most solemn passover that was ever celebrated upon earth, received no other consecration than that which the presence of those distinguished guests supplied. No priests, or other officials, preceded that wonderful celebration; and to this day it remains an undisputed fact that where that first bread was broken, and where that first hymn was sung,—that sweet chant, in which the voice of "God, manifest in the flesh," took his full part,—even there no priest consecrated, and consecration was never invoked! Blush ye modern ecclesiastics, that ye wrangle about a consecration to which the great Redeemer of the world paid no kind of heed!*

The whole question of consecration was never more fully, or more candidly, discussed than during the impeachment of Archbishop Laud; and as it is given at considerable length by Neal, the following summary of his statements will assist the reader in forming a safe judgment of the entire controversy.

The archbishop was charged, among other things, with a "superstitious manner of consecrating chapels, churches, and churchyards, and his accusers instanced in particular his consecration in St. Catharine Cree Church, and in St. Giles's-in-the-Fields.† They objected, further, that he

* See Mark xiv. 15, and Luke xxii. 12. *Dr. Doddridge*, on Acts ii. 2, seems to think that "the upper room," where the apostles "used to meet," was the scene of the outpouring of the Holy Spirit on the day of Pentecost. If so (and it is strongly probable), there is no proof that it was ever "consecrated."

† For the consecration of these churches, see Appendix A.

consecrated altars, with all their furniture, as chalices, altar cloths, and even the knife that was to cut the sacramental bread. To these charges the archbishop replied that the practice was as ancient as Moses, who consecrated the tabernacle, with all its vessels and ornaments; that King Solomon afterwards consecrated the temple; and that in the reign of Constantine the Great, churches were consecrated, and so it has continued down to the present time." The Commons' managers (who were his official accusers) replied, that if the tabernacle was consecrated, it was by Moses, the civil magistrate, and not by Aaron, the high priest; that the temple was consecrated by the king himself, and not by the high priest; that the only consecration of the tabernacle and its utensils was by anointing them with oil, for which Moses had received an express command; and that the consecration of the temple was but by Solomon's offering an excellent prayer in the outward court, and *not in the temple itself*. But, they added, even allowing that the temple was consecrated in an extraordinary manner, there is no mention, either in Scripture or in the Jewish writers, of the consecration of their synagogues, to which our churches properly succeed; and, after all, it is no conclusive way of arguing, to derive a Christian institution from the Jewish church, many of whose ordinances were but temporary, and were abolished by the coming of Christ. As to the beginning of Christianity, they affirmed that for three hundred years there was no credible authority for the consecration of churches, and the case mentioned in connection with Constantine was an erection over the Saviour's sepulchre at Jerusalem; but there it was done by prayers, disputations, preaching, and exposition of Scripture; but there were no processions, no knocking at the doors by the bishop; no reverencing towards the altar; and no pronouncing the ground holy; all of which things were unknown in the Christian church till the very darkest times of Popery."*

Whatever may be thought of the comparative merits of the disputants in the foregoing discussion, one statement by the "managers" is beyond all doubt or cavil, and that is, "that *for about three hundred years* there was no credible authority for the consecration of churches." This statement is confirmed in substance by the most reliable ecclesiastical historians, whom it may be considered expedient to consult.

Dr. Cave, with characteristic modesty, says of the practice—"When it was first taken up by Christians is not easy to determine, only I do not remember to have met with the footsteps of any such thing in any approved writer, till the reign of Constantine. In his time Christianity having become more prosperous and successful, churches were everywhere erected and repaired; and no sooner were so, but they were solemnly consecrated, and the dedications celebrated with great festivity and rejoicing." After referring to the instances of this, at Tyre and at Jerusalem, he goes on to remark that the annual commemoration of these dedications "much prevailed in after ages, some shadow whereof still remains amongst us at this day, in the wakes observed in several counties, which are annual festivals kept in country villages in memory of the dedication of their particular churches."†

* *History of the Puritans.* Vol. ii., pp. 303, 4, 5.

† *Primitive Christianity.* Chap. vi., pp. 72, 3.

Gibbon substantially confirms the above, and says that "till this period (A.D. 260) they (the Christians) had usually held their assemblies in private houses and sequestered places. They were now permitted to erect and consecrate convenient edifices for the purpose of religious worship."* The learned Mede says of the places of worship used by the apostles that "they were some capable and convenient room within the walls or dwelling of some pious disciple, dedicated by the religious bounty of the owner to the use of the church, and that usually an upper room, being, according to their manner of building, the most large and capacious of any other, so likewise the most retired and freest from disturbance, and next to heaven, as having no other room above it."†

Bingham, the most industrious, and usually the most accurate of our writers on *Antiquities of the Christian Church*, fails to add anything to the above, but leaves in considerable doubt the origin of *churches* as separate buildings, and devolves the question at large on mere inferences that are far from conclusive.‡

§ II.—CONSECRATION OF PERSONS.

"The motives that ought to determine a man to dedicate himself to the church, are a zeal for promoting the glory of God, and for raising the honour of the Christian religion. This man, and only this man, so moved or qualified, can, in truth, and with a good conscience, answer that he TRUSTS *he is inwardly moved by the Holy*

* *Decline and Fall.* Vol. i., chap. 16, p. 330, and note.

† *Quoted in Bates's "College Lectures,"* p. 45.

‡ *Antiquities.* Book 8, pp. 277-9.

Ghost: and every one that ventures on the saying it without this, is a sacrilegious profaner of the name of God and his Holy Spirit; he breaks in upon the church not to feed, but to rob it."*

Bishop Burnet is by no means too severe in this solemn condemnation of official hypocrisy, for nothing tends more directly to the ruin of immortal souls than a deceptive ministry. The streams of salvation are thus polluted, if not absolutely poisoned, before they reach the lips of the people, and the community at large are then left without hope "and without God in the world."† Nothing can be more fatal to a nation's religion than to have teachers who profess to be "moved by the Holy Ghost" to preach the gospel, but who are total strangers to the work of that blessed Spirit upon their own hearts. Strong as the bishop's language may be, it is not less true than strong, to say of such men that they "break in upon the church, not to feed, but to rob it."

But how does the Church of England meet the case? Is it, as it ought to be, by a close examination into the religious *experience* of its ministerial candidates, with a view to the rejection of carnal, worldly, unconverted men? Is the formulary employed adapted, or even *intended*, to effect this scrutiny of character, and by such a course to preserve the church of God from the intrusion of selfish men, whose chief aim is to enter a genteel profession, or to obtain the emoluments of an office that none but heaven-taught ministers of religion have any right to sustain? Let the form speak for itself, and let every candid reader say whether it does not partake far more of

* Burnet's "Pastoral Care," p. 96. † Ephesians ii. 12.

clerical presumption than of any fitness to search out character, and to keep the unworthy from entering the sacred fold.

Towgood puts the subject with becoming seriousness, in these words :—" When the bishop lays his hands on the student's head, then kneeling before him, and makes this solemn address : *Receive the Holy Ghost. Whose sins thou dost forgive, they are forgiven ; and whose sins thou dost retain, they are retained ; in the name of the Father, of the Son, and of the Holy Ghost. Amen.* Is this a language which can be clearly justified ? Do their lordships keep perfectly free of the offence which Bishop Burnet so justly condemns ? Is there nothing like *lying to the Holy Ghost* in the part which they are called to act in this most serious affair ? "*

Without charging upon the consecrating bishops, that, as Towgood puts it, they are guilty of " lying to the Holy Ghost," it may be asked with the utmost possible propriety, have they the power, under any known circumstances, of conferring the Holy Ghost at all ? Can they give that over which they have no control whatever ? And what does the act of " consecration " amount to if, after all, the Holy Ghost is not given ? Is the act, with all its solemn and imposing circumstantials, anything short of a delusion and a snare ? And this is but taking low ground in the face of the tremendous powers with which it assumes to invest the candidate, who possibly is hardly more than a boy just out of his " teens "—namely, those of remitting or retaining sin, which are prerogatives exclusively divine, and far too sacred and too

* Towgood's " Dissent Justified," p. 265.

awful to be lodged in human hands. That mortal men—even officials of the highest class—possess themselves, and can impart to others, these terrible prerogatives is, upon the face of it, an assumption equally at variance with Christian humility and the teachings of the Word of God. The apostles never professed an authority so awful, and the best ages of the church were those in which it was wholly unknown.

And no support whatever can be derived to this amazing claim from the disputed and yet unproved plea of an "*apostolic succession*," since any such plea concedes to the Papacy an unbroken official sanctity, that includes such monsters as a Sergius III., John XII., and Benedict IX.* Such a succession, could it be proved, would generate contempt, rather than confer the slightest honour; and the veriest tyro in ecclesiastical history would regard the plea as a public disgrace. The true "apostolic succession" is one of *character* exclusively, succession to office being an utter impossibility, since none but the twelve apostles themselves ever saw Christ face to face.† That this was a condition of apostleship is evident, first, from the remarkable qualification demanded by the apostles in the successor to Judas Iscariot (one of the twelve), that one must be ordained in his room, "to be a witness with us of his resurrection;" and, secondly, from the special revelation made of himself by the Saviour to Saul of Tarsus when on his way to Damascus, in order properly to qualify him

* 'History of the Christian Church,' by G. Gregory, D.D. Vol. ii., pp. 5, 9, 40.

† This, of course, excepts the "above five hundred brethren at once" (1 Cor. xv. 6), and others, who never claimed to be apostles.

for the apostleship. Of this qualification the apostle afterwards availed himself, when some among the cavilling Corinthians questioned his claim to that distinguished office, and he wrote thus :—" Am I not an apostle ? *Have I not seen Jesus Christ our Lord ?* " One chief design of the apostolic appointments was to bear witness to the resurrection, and to testify to the world that He who died upon the Cross was alive again ; but when this testimony had been given to the world by those who had seen " him alive after death," the apostolic office ceased, and the " succession " came to a final close. From that period to the present time the rule of the church has been, " Yea, though we have known Christ *after the flesh*, yet now henceforth know we him no more ; " and the corresponding proof of true Christian character, down to the end of time, is given in the words of Peter, " Whom *having not seen*, ye love ; in whom, though now *ye see him not*, yet believing, ye rejoice with joy unspeakable and full of glory."* With the close of the apostolic *office* the *special* gifts also ceased ; hence the professed power to give the Holy Spirit now, must be regarded as nothing better than a popular delusion.

This view of " apostolic succession " receives strong confirmation from the recorded practice of the church in the earliest and purest ages of Christianity. Neander, with his usual clearness and research, gives, at considerable length, the opinions of Tertullian on this point, of which this is a summary :—" He charged his opponents with attributing to men a power that belonged only to God ; that Christ had not delivered any such power to the

* Acts i. 22 ; 1 Cor. ix. 1 ; 1 Peter i. 8 ; 2 Cor. v. 16.

church,—certainly not to the bishops,—and hence, if they arrogated to themselves such a power, it must have appeared to him as venturing to assume a power which belonged to God alone. The bishops regarded themselves as the successors of the apostles, and, through Peter, as the representatives of apostolic power. Tertullian, on the contrary, maintained that the bishops were the successors of the apostles, only in reference to the exercise of their office as teachers, not in reference to the spiritual power delivered to them; he further contended that if the bishops wished to be successors of the apostles in this respect, they must prove it by similar instances of divine power, the ability to work miracles, and to foretell future events; and he made a bold appeal to whoever might claim this power to forgive sins, "Show me, then, thou successor of the apostles, who or what thou art to forgive sins, thou who showest thyself to be neither prophet nor apostle, and wantest that power which is needed to forgive sin?"*

An able writer in the 'Faiths of the World,' who appears to have devoted much patient attention to the subject of absolution, after giving a brief history of the practice in its connection with the various churches, remarks—"The question naturally arises, however, at what period in the history of the church was the indicative form introduced, 'I absolve thee,' instead of the deprecatory form 'May God or Christ absolve thee?' Morinus, in his work 'De Pœnitentia,' has satisfactorily proved that the indicative form was altogether unknown until *the twelfth or thirteenth* century, not long before the time of Thomas Aquinas, who was one of the first who

* 'History of the Planting of Christianity.' Vol. ii., pp. 394, 5.

wrote in defence of it. Ever since, this form of absolution has prevailed in the Romish church."*

Coleman, in his excellent work on 'Christian Antiquities,' observes that "no established form of absolution is recorded, but from analogy it might be presumed that some such was in use. Nothing like the modern method of absolving in the name of the Father, Son, and Holy Ghost, was known to the ancient church."†

These authorities, with others that might be adduced, prove conclusively that the modern custom of absolution was unknown to the early Christian church; that more than a thousand years elapsed before its present form was attempted; and that the Protestant Church of England has accepted its baseless pretensions exclusively from the Church of Rome, without any authority whatever from the Word of God.

§ III.—The Consecration of Churchyards and Burying-Grounds.

"The burying places of the Greeks and Romans were at a distance from their towns; and the Jews had their sepulchres in gardens and in fields. *The present practice was introduced by the clergy, who pretended that the dead enjoyed peculiar privileges by being interred in consecrated ground.*"‡

An unusual importance just now attaches to the question of "consecrated ground," from the melancholy fact

* Faiths of the World.—The word *Absolution.*

† 'Christian Antiquities.' Chap. 17, sect. 5.

‡ 'Haydn's Dictionary of Dates,' p. 145.—See Matt. xxvii. 60; John xix. 41.

that an invidious and utterly useless distinction is carried by official assumption to the borders of the grave—even to the very brink of eternity! Surely there must be something grievously wrong—something profoundly vicious—in a system that supports and defends a practice that stops but one step short of making the everlasting happiness, the awful future of eternity, to depend upon the kind of "ground" in which dead bodies are laid! The distinction, for which some parties contend, even to episcopal wrath, ought to bear on its front the impress of heaven, and be ready to show that the "consecrated" privilege comes direct from the Holy Bible, and can be proved to be divine from the word of the living God! Nothing short of this will meet the case, or prevent the claim of "consecrated ground" from being regarded as a delusion, imposed upon the world by "the Man of Sin," or an "invention," that only Popery, in its worst phases, could have produced. If this "consecrated ground" is not authorized by Holy Scripture, by some express command, or by fair and honest inference, then is it anything less than an imposition on public credulity, and a mode of deception for which there can be no imaginable excuse? At the grave, at least, all the paltry distinctions of time ought to cease, and the system, be it where it may, that carries such distinctions to the brink of eternity, should be driven from among Christian men without delay.

It makes the matter all the more to be deplored when it is remembered that this unnecessary annoyance is sanctioned by devoted clergymen, who, in all other respects, are the true "salt of the earth," and who, for sound doctrine, holy conversation, and sincere attachment to the

Redeemer's interests, are not excelled by any class of officials throughout the land. That such men as these can deliberately maintain this uncalled-for distinction at a time when the consolations of religion should be supplied to the bereaved and the sorrowing, is an inconsistency that falls but little short of a public disgrace! Let such men ask themselves how such conduct will appear before the bar of God?*

* Who can read such statements as the following without blushing for the dishonour done to the Christian name, and that too by men who, above all others, are pledged to "weep with them that weep?":— "Much scandal has been created at Oxford recently by the refusal of the curate of St. Thomas parish to allow a corpse (that of a female), to be interred or brought into the cemetery, unless the friends submitted to the funeral service of the Church of England being performed over the body, although the deceased, who was a member of a Nonconformist Church, had expressed a very decided wish that it should not be done, and a service had already been performed at her own chapel, in conformity with the wish of the deceased and the members of her family. Finding that he would not allow the interment to proceed unless he performed the service, rather than return with the corpse the husband of the deceased submitted, under strong protest, to what they termed a piece of clerical tyranny."

"At a meeting of clergy, lately, at Plymouth, the following resolutions were passed:—That, in the opinion of this Chapter, the most strenuous opposition should be used to prevent the passing of any Burials' Bill, similar to Mr. Osborne Morgan's measure of 1875, or any bill which treats our churchyards as national rather than ecclesiastical property. That the Burials' Act be further extended, so that increased facilities be given for the formation of public cemeteries where required. That this Chapter would not oppose the burial of Nonconformists in the churchyards silently and without any service under due regulations and safeguards."

This obstinate determination to adhere to a supposed privilege is

"In the beginning of the sixth century," says Bingham, "the people also seem to have been admitted to the same privilege of being buried in the *atrium*, or churchyard, before the church; but still they were forbidden, by laws both ecclesiastical and civil, to bury in the church."* Coleman makes a similar statement in these words:— "About the sixth century it became customary to use the *churchyard* as a burial place. In some instances it was so used as early as the fourth century."† Dr. Eadie is more particular still, and says—"About the fourth century enclosures round churches began to be employed for burial grounds; at first exclusively for ecclesiastical dignitaries, afterwards for any who died in the communion of the church; *but there is no example of a proper consecration of these before the sixth century*, nor of burial within churches before the ninth."‡ The council of Braga, in Spain, which was held about A.D. 563, gave permission to bury, if necessary, in the churchyard under the walls of the church, and the custom gradually spread to other countries; but even then there was no "consecration," and the first writer who mentions that ceremony is Gregory, of Tours, in A.D. 570. "So long as the law was in force throughout the Roman empire, the Christians, in compliance with it, were obliged to bury their dead without the gates of the city, a custom which prevailed here in England till about the middle of the *eighth century*, when Archbishop Cuthbert, of Canterbury, obtained a

only adapted to make Christians weep and infidels rejoice. "Charity seeketh not her own," but such men know it not.

* 'Antiquities.' Book xxiii., chap. 1. † 'Antiquities.' Chap. 9, sec. 7.

‡ 'Ecclesiastical Cyclopædia,' p. 111.

dispensation from the Pope for making churchyards within the walls."* "The ancients," says the Rev. Thomas Hartwell Horne, "had not that indecent and unwholesome custom, which now prevails, of crowding all their dead in the midst of their towns and cities, within the narrow precincts of *a place reputed sacred*, much less of amassing them in the bosom of their fanes and temples. The burying places of the Romans were at a distance from their towns; and the Jews had their sepulchres in gardens, in fields, and in the sides of mountains."† "It was an ancient custom," as Dr. David Jennings remarks, "to bury the dead under trees, or in woods. Deborah (Genesis xxxv. 8) was buried under an oak near Bethel; and the bones of Saul and Jonathan under a tree at Jabesh" (1 Saml. xxxi. 13), from which it plainly appears that the "consecration" of burying places was wholly unknown to the Jews.‡

It is not necessary to multiply authorities in so clear a case, for those now given are amply sufficient for the purpose, and they establish the following points:—First, that the primitive Christians—*the Christians of the three first centuries*—knew nothing whatever of "consecration, or even of churchyards;" and, secondly, that the ceremony of "consecration" of places for the dead sprang up in the *sixth century*, and not before. It follows, therefore, as a consequence that the "consecration" of churchyards, or of other burying places for the dead, has no sanction at all from holy Scripture, and possesses no kind of claim

* Wheatley on the 'Book of Common Prayer,' chap. 12, sec. 2.

† Horne's 'Introduction to the Bible.' Vol. iii., part 4, chap. 8.

‡ See Appendix B.

on the attention of Christians. It was never appointed by the blessed God, but is the production of priestly pride alone; and that which adds to the sadness of the case is, that there are men to be found who will persist in maintaining the unauthorised claim, at the expense of the tenderest feelings of our common humanity, and that too at a time when hearts are overwhelmed with sorrow, and bowed down under the heaviest possible grief! Why this is persisted in it is difficult to understand, except for the "fees!"

§ IV.—The "Consecration" of Banners, Flags, and other Material Employed in War.

"*Blessed are the peacemakers*" is a divine benediction, whose beauty and loveliness are above all human praise, and beyond all mortal conception. It breathes of heaven, and smiles with a sweetness to which our jarring world can supply no parallel from any of its schools of morals, or any of the philosophies that have instructed and enlightened the successive ages of mankind. Its unadorned simplicity and the majestic ease with which it glides into all the diversified affairs of men are unquestionable proofs of its divine and heavenly origin, while its obvious purpose in the promotion of the happiness of all mankind, stamps it with an excellence that no merely human law can ever reach. Within the same compass of words there is no blessing pronounced so rich, so felicitous, or so comprehensive.

But does war in any of its phases, or in any part of its vast machinery or *insignia*, accord with this sacred benediction? Would any official, whether lay or cleric, who has consented to consecrate a war banner, or standard, or ship of war, ever dare to connect with the religious ceremony in which he must occupy a leading position, the Saviour's divine words, and say to the troops, the officers, or the crew around him, "Blessed are the peacemakers?" The two things are so utterly incompatible—so reverse the one from the other—that it would expose the man to universal ridicule and contempt who should attempt the impossible task. They are

"Wide as the poles asunder,"

and the deep-rooted consciousness of this has never allowed the attempt to appear among the numerous absurdities of mankind. But what does this systematic silence prove, other than that the "consecration" of war material in any shape or form is at variance with Christianity, and that he who blesses war banners and the like, dares not, on the ground of the commonest consistency, utter the divine benediction, "Blessed are the peacemakers." The one act is that of dignifying a blind brute force, but the other breathes out the noblest aspiration of reason in pronouncing the highest blessing on peacemakers, who "shall be called the children of God."

It will give an insight into this system of war-consecration to submit a few instances of its actual performance, as reported in the public journals of the various periods in which the events took place.

In the year 1841 new colours were presented to the 73rd Regiment, at Gosport, in the presence of Major-General Sir Hercules Pakenham, Lady Pakenham, and a large number of "the fashionables of the neighbourhood." On that occasion the venerable Archdeacon Wilberforce (afterwards Bishop Wilberforce), delivered a warlike speech in these words :—" Gallant men of the 73rd, we are this day gathered here together for no ordinary purpose; you are brought here in the presence of these your countrymen, under the eye of distinguished commanders, to receive from the hands of the fairest amongst us,* the new colours which your Queen commits to your keeping; and here you are met by the ministers of Christ's church—by the special servants of the Prince of Peace. And for what is it we meet you here? Not merely to add to the pageant of this gala day; not merely to swell the tidings of high and noble feelings which the glorious sight of your disciplined ranks and gallant bearing must have called up in the coldest heart amongst us. It is not for this that we are here; we dare not, for such purposes as this, take into our lips the awful name we bear with us and bless you in His name. But we are here, and meet you this day, that we may impress on you, and on all around us, a great moral lesson,—a lesson that you never should forget, —the lesson of your true dignity as Christian soldiers. For of a Christian army we dare not deem as of a mere gathering of brute force, be it never so mighty; nor may you so deem of yourselves. It is not your admirable discipline; it is not your practised evolutions; it is not your approved courage; it is not even, wonderful as it is, the simple unity of action which pervades your various multitude, which should be your glory as a Christian army. It is, that you are the maintainers of right—the avengers of wrong; it is that you are God's instruments in the government of this world; that you fight not for lust of

* Lady Pakenham.

power, nor for lust of gold, nor for a vile and murderous ambition, but to uphold the truth for the liberties of that land which God has given you for your country, for your fathers' graves, for your mothers' honour, for your children's freedom, for the church's welfare, for your Queen, your faith, and your God. This is the honour of a Christian army; and this, therefore, is the reason why we meet you here this day. This is why those colours, which are soon to float upon the breeze which echoes with your martial music, which are to lead you on to victory in the din and the carnage of the battle field, now lie before you in the form of that holy cross, in which is all the hope of your salvation. This is why we meet you here in the name of our God, and bless you as his minister. May the great moral lesson sink into your heart; may you not forget that you are Christian men in thinking yourselves soldiers; but remember you are therefore soldiers because you are most truly Christian men. Remember, therefore, that forgetfulness of God, is forgetting your true character; it is losing the high office which you bear, in the frivolities of thoughtfulness, or the brute efforts of a savage recklessness. The fear of God is the true basis of all courage and work as His instruments; remember that we fight for truth and righteousness and peace; that the wars of Christian nations are a final and awful appeal to the justice of the God of battles. This it is which gives to those names emblazoned on your colours their true and bright effulgence;* this it is which has cast around the name of Waterloo its imperishable glory; this is why it should be handed on to the children of your

* 'Seringapatam,' 'Mangalore,' 'Waterloo.'

children's children, as a household word of British honour; this is why our hearts warmed at the remembrance of your brave commanders in arms, who slept upon that field the sleep of glory; this is why our spirits stir when we look at the trophies and the wounds of those who bled with you that day; this is why we bid you think upon it often; hereafter you may do in turn such deeds yourselves. Not because we won a hard-fought and famous action, but because we fought for truth, and triumphed in the cause of God and man; because we stood the shock of that battle-field; not for the vulgar laurels of fame or empire, but because we fought for the rights, the liberty of all the world, against the wilful king of violence, the fierce and selfish despiser of the happiness and welfare of humanity. Therefore is that name of Waterloo dear to British ears; therefore at this sound do British hearts warm within them; therefore must it be for years to come the British soldier's watchword. This great moral lesson, soldiers of the 73rd, would we this day imprint upon your deepest memory; therefore do we meet you here; therefore do we bless you in the name of God; therefore do we call upon you now to join in solemn prayer to Him, whose blessing we would earnestly implore on you who are to bear these banners, on all those who shall hereafter stand around them in the fight, on our country and our Queen."

The Archdeacon then offered the following prayer:—

"Let us Pray.

"O Lord of hosts, who art God of the armies of heaven, and amongst the inhabitants of the earth, look down, we beseech thee, upon us, thy most unworthy servants, who come before thee in the name of Jesus Christ our Lord, and extend to us thine accustomed favour and protection. Bless, O Lord, this day, the works of our hands; yea, prosper thou our handiwork. Hear us as thou art wont; hear us, O Lord, as thou didst hear thy people of Israel in the old time. Yea, be thou with us as thou wast with Joshua upon the plains of Jericho, and by the waters of Merom. Accept this offering of ourselves and ours to thee, and be thou amongst us the Captain of the host of the Lord; yea, as the living God. Grant, O Lord, that, as a people we may fear thee, and put our trust in thee. Bless with thine especial blessings our most gracious sovereign Lady Queen Victoria, with her royal consort and their noble issue. Bless her person and her crown with every spiritual and earthly blessing; may she reign long and gloriously in the loyal hearts of this great people; guide thou all her counsels by thy godly wisdom; may her armies and her navies glorify thy name and uphold her rights—may her soldiers and her sailors, with loyal English hearts, love, honour, and serve her as the Lord's anointed—may they make her name great, as their fathers have made great the names of those who sat before her on the throne of her progenitors. Go thou forth before us, O thou God of battles, in the day of battle. May we ever fight for truth and righteousness and peace, and do thou defend the right—make our soldiers brave and merciful, temperate and faithful, resolute and daring.

"Bless especially, we pray thee, these thy servants; govern them in the day of battle; may these banners, which we bless and consecrate this day, lead them on to glorious victory—may they always be unfurled in the cause of truth and right for our Queen, our country, and our God. May the remembrance of the great things thou hast done for us, thy servants, in the times of old, fill our hearts with self-abasement, and with trust in thee. We know, O Lord, that it is not in our own might, but in thy present help, that we are strong. To thy name, O Lord, be all the praise: we deserve not the least of all thy mercies; we have sinned with our fathers, and done very wickedly. Deal not with us, Lord, according to our sins: cast us not off though we have trespassed against thee; but for thy dear Son's sake continue thy favour and thy mercies to us. Cleanse thou our arms from unrighteous blood. Be thou in the midst of our hosts, as thou wast in the plains of India and on the field of Waterloo. Grant that these banners, which we raise this day, and here commit to these brave men, thy servants, may be ever maintained by courageous hearts, and held up by arms of strength; cover thou the heads of their defenders in the day of battle: be thou their buckler and the strength of their arm; grant them in the hottest fight to fix their hopes on thee, and in the time of victory and triumph to give thanks to thee and magnify thy name; that serving thee here on earth with faithfulness and loyal bravery, fighting daily in the strength of thy Holy Spirit against their ghostly enemy, following ever more in holy living the Captain of our salvation, they may so fight the better fight of faith, that in thy good time they may be received unto the rest and peace of thy eternal and heavenly kingdom, for the alone merit's sake of him who died for us, Jesus Christ, thy Son, our Lord."*

* See Appendix C.

About the same period, colours were presented to the 72nd Highlanders, at Windsor, by the Duke of Wellington, whose modest address, contrasting advantageously with that of Archdeacon Wilberforce, was reported in the *Times* in these words:—"By the invitation of your commanding officer, and with the gracious permission of her Majesty, I have the greatest satisfaction in appearing before you on this occasion to present to this regiment a new stand of colours. These colours have been consecrated by *one of the highest dignitaries of the church*, and they are presented to you in the presence of a number of most illustrious personages, in the presence of her Majesty's illustrious guest, the King of Prussia, who has in his service some of the finest troops in Europe, in the presence of his royal highness the Prince Albert, and of many other distinguished officers."

The officiating "dignitary" on this occasion was Dr. Sumner, Bishop of Winchester, who, while far less fulsome and bombastical than Archdeacon Wilberforce, was fully his equal in ignoring the Christian truth, that "the weapons of our warfare are not carnal, but mighty through God to the pulling down of strongholds," and he closed a long and war-inspiring speech in these words:—"Be ready to fight unto the death, at your Queen's bidding, for her honour, for your country, and your God; but be ever mindful of that far higher warfare, in which you, in common with us all, are bound, as Christian men, as well as Christian soldiers, to strive for the victory. And then, in the language of the admonition addressed at investiture to the knights of that most noble order of which I bear the badge, 'May you so overpass both prosperous and adverse encounters, that, having stoutly vanquished your enemies, both of body and soul, you may not only receive the praise of this transient combat, but be crowned with the palm of eternal victory.'"

A similar scene was enacted at Athlone, in 1842, then the quarters of the 32nd Regiment, and the ceremony was performed by the Rev. H. Murray, the incumbent of St. Peter's, who concluded his prayer in these words :—"*May these banners, which we now bless and consecrate in thy name, be preserved with honour*;" and his whole address was one that encouraged killing men, "in the cause of the sovereign and the country."

Archdeacon Musgrave accepted the same office for the Second West York Yeomanry, at Halifax, about the same time. He, however, admitted the existence of "misguided" but "benevolent men," who denied the *lawfulness of war*, yet he adduced no argument to prove its lawfulness, and quoted no single passage of Holy Scripture in support of a system that has spread "battle, murder, and sudden death" all over the world.

Scenes such as these are fearful enough at home in England, surrounded as they ever will be by counteracting influences of a pacific tendency; but what must not be their disastrous effects on the native mind in such a country as India, where the people naturally look up to their Christian conquerors for an example better than their own? Yet both at Moulmein and Calcutta "presentations" of colours took place; the one by the Bishop of Calcutta, and the other by that well-known warrior Sir Charles Napier. In the former instance the bishop, as usual, offered up the consecrating prayer, and, after an introduction, he proceeded thus:—"We implore thy blessing upon our sovereign lady Queen Victoria, *and the Honourable the East India Company*, and upon Her Majesty's arms in every part of the world, and especially in British India. We offer and present unto thee, O Lord, these banners, and beseech thee ever to bless them and all those who shall march under them, wherever they may be borne. Be pleased at this time to accept, O Lord, this our dedication of these banners to thy high and glorious Majesty," &c. Sir Charles Napier does not appear to have attempted prayer, but, as a veteran warrior, he contented himself with an address to the troops (the 1st Bombay Fusileers), which contained neither peace nor inconsistency. He made no vaunting profession of being "the minister of the Prince of Peace," while he prompted the soldiers to be bold in deeds of bloodshed; and if he said nothing proper to a bishop or an archdeacon, he said nothing inconsistent with the profession of the sword. He closed his address with these warlike words:—"Take your splendid colours, soldiers, refulgent with the glories of a hundred battles! Ye are as good men, as brave men, and as strong men to do battle as the heroes who went before you, and shall renovate your fame as you have this day renovated your standards!"

The repulsive inconsistency between the prayers and the profession of the ministers of the gospel of peace, as given above, has produced an amount of disgust from time time, that finds vent in various ways, to the great dishonour of the "consecrating clergy" at large, and to the injury of the Christian religion as a system professing to consult and aim at, the good of all mankind. "How can such a religion be what it claims to be—the remedy for human misery all over the world—when its pledged officials actually 'consecrate' war banners, and earnestly pray for their success, though representing destruction and death also, all over the world?" This is the inquiry of thoughtful men in various directions; and it remains for the "consecrating" clergy to supply an answer that shall preserve the Christian faith from the taunt of the sceptic and the sneer of the infidel. One of these questioners, said to be a man of some literary repute, was so appalled at the inconsistency of the practice that he prepared a suitable prayer for the occasion, of which the following is a copy:—

"O Lord of Hosts, smile upon thy servants now marshalled before thee for the work of death. Breathe into them, O God of War, the spirit of their profession. Let them for the time forget thy prohibition of old, *Thou shalt not kill*, and also those commands of thy gospel which bid them do good unto all men, to love even their enemies, and turn the other cheek to the smiter. Thou knowest, Omniscient Father of all, this is no time for the application of such principles; and we pray thee to animate them with sentiments more appropriate to the awful duties of this hour, and thus prepare them for a glorious and signal triumph over their enemies. Fill them with the spirit of war, and enable them, in humble reliance on thee, to shoot and stab and trample down their foes. Nerve every arm; direct every blow; guide every sword, every bayonet, every bullet, to the seat of life, that we may soon reap a glorious harvest of death. . . . Fight, then, for us, and give thy servants a great victory, for which all the people shall praise thee."

The ill-concealed sarcasm of this prayer is open to grave censure; but, notwithstanding this, neither hypocrisy nor inconsistency can be charged upon it; and, apart from its warlike terms, it would far better become the "consecration of colours," than the one offered by Archdeacon Wilberforce at Gosport.

The Mahommedan and the Jew are equally severe in their taunts against the inconsistency of the *Christian* advocates of war, both lay and cleric, as the following statements too painfully prove:—"When a Christian missionary, armed with the authority and the humility of the Gospel, was conversing with a follower of the prophet, within sight of the mountain of Calvary, where the Prince of Peace laid down his life, in order that he might open the gates of Paradise for a fallen race,— 'Why do you come to us?' asked the Mahommedan. 'To bring you peace,' was the reply. 'Peace!' exclaimed the Mahommedan; 'look at that hill; there, upon that very spot where your Lord poured out his blood, even the Mahommedan is obliged to interfere, to prevent Christians from shedding the blood of each other.'"

A pious clergyman of the Established Church, having been announced to preach at Falmouth for the Society for the Conversion of the Jews, was answered by the following striking address, affixed to the church-door:—

"Our Messiah, when he comes, will establish a system of mercy, peace, and kindness upon earth; while among you Christians, nothing but disputes, animosities, and cruelties mark your passage through the world. Possibly your religion sanctions these things: ours does not; for with us the goodness and beneficence alone of the Mosaic laws constitute their grand authority, and proclaim aloud their emanation from a good and beneficent God. We want no better; we expect no better, until the Messiah shall indeed come. Then (if the prophets of our Sacred Volume speak true) the conduct of a man towards his fellows will be the reverse of what it is now. 'Every man shall then sit under his own vine, and under his own fig-tree; nation shall no longer lift up sword against nation, neither shall they learn war any more; but the leopard shall lie down with the kid; the wolf and the lamb feed together, and a little child shall lead them.' Has this happy period, this golden era of public peace and private love, ever yet been witnessed? Speak candidly, Christian, has it been once seen through the last 1800 years?

"Your brother of the dust,

"ZECKER LACHORCAN.*

"Tizri, 5823."

On a calm review of the foregoing display of "consecrating" industry, it will be apparent to every thoughtful reader that the piety exhibited is little, if anything, short of profanity itself, and that some of the statements make a near approach to awful blasphemy. For once the writer feels it his solemn duty to be plain, and as the honour of our noble Christianity is infinitely more important than the transient reputation of any of its officials, whatever be their rank or station, he must be permitted to express an honest opinion upon a practice so utterly at variance with the religion of love to all mankind.

To say nothing of the laboured turgidity and jejuneness of the address of Archdeacon Wilberforce, is it not a manifest delusion (to use no stronger term), to say to a number of men of whose moral character he could know nothing at all, "You are therefore soldiers, *because you are*

* Herald of Peace, 1828, pp. 347, 8.

most truly Christian men!" Or, in the spirit of an empty, but irritating boast, to feed the vanity of the same men, by assuring them that Waterloo "must be for years to come *the British soldier's watchword!*" Is this to preach forgiveness? or to "overcome evil with good?" Can a strain of address so entirely opposed to the charity that is not "puffed up" ever serve the cause of Him who was "meek and lowly in heart?" As to the archdeacon's prayer, where, throughout its entire length, is there one solitary petition at all like that taught us by the Great Redeemer, "And forgive us our trespasses, *as we also forgive them that trespass against us?*" Is not the retention of "Waterloo" in open defiance of such a prayer?

The other addresses require no particular remark, except that their spirit contradicts the declaration, "Peace on earth, goodwill to men;" but an expression in the prayer of Mr. Murray, at Athlone, calls for a stern rebuke, and it is the one already quoted—"May these banners, which we now bless and consecrate *in Thy name*, be preserved with honour." Had that clergyman forgotten the denunciation of the great moral law that "the Lord will not hold him guiltless that taketh his name in vain?" Has that divine being ever authorised any man to attach His sacred name to war banners, for the purpose of sanctifying deeds of hatred and strife? Where has He given permission to fallible men to pronounce His holy name upon the machinery and embellishments of a system that springs from the "lusts that war in our members?"* To employ the gentlest phrase possible to the case, it is nothing less than a vain pretence,

* James iv. 1.

if not a daring blasphemy, so to degrade "the God of Peace,"* as to apply His awful name to banners and "colours" that are deliberately intended to *adorn* the most ferocious scenes that can disgrace the reason and destroy the happiness of rational man! Let such divines remember that in the solemn judgment to come, "The Lord will not hold him 'guiltless' that taketh His name in vain;" nor should they forget that "it is a fearful thing to fall into the hands of the living God;" and that "He is not mocked, but whatsoever a man soweth that shall he also reap." That "reaping" time is a fearful prospect for those who have encouraged deeds of blood. "*God is love*," is the sublime description of the Great Supreme,—the God and Father of us all,—and, *without an express appointment*, as in Jewish days, will any mortal man dare the profane act of pronouncing the name of the infinite "*Love*" upon instruments of cruelty, destruction, and death? Sooner than such a deed should be sanctioned and encouraged by *Christian* ministers, one feels ready to exclaim, "May creation sink into oblivion, and be remembered no more!"

The exact period when this unscriptural practice of "consecrating" war appendages commenced is far from being clear; but it is evident beyond all doubt or questioning, that while the Jews had their banners in a very early age, yet these were never employed for war purposes, and the *consecration* of such tribe distinctions was wholly unknown. "Banners were common to all nations. The Jewish tribes had standards or banners—Num. ii. The standard of Constantine bore the inscription, *In hoc signo vinces*—"In

* Romans xv. 33.

this sign thou shalt conquer," under the figure of a cross. The flag is said to have been introduced by the Saracens, before whose time the ensigns of war were extended on cross pieces of wood; but the practice in the army of using a cross on standards and shields arose from the example of Constantine, whose *miraculous* assumption of that sign took place in the fourth century, and not earlier.* "Colours, standards, and military ensigns of various kinds, to distinguish the different corps in an army, and to animate them with courage in defence of their insignia, appear to have been of great antiquity in all countries, and were not unknown to the ancient Britons. The standard of Fingal, which was called the Sunbeam, is described with great pomp in the poems of Ossian."† The first notice of banners in England is in Bede's account of the interview between Augustine and King Ethelbert; the monasteries had their banners; the Pope still sends *consecrated* banners where he wishes success; and English ecclesiastics appear to have borrowed their practice from the Romish church; and the "consecration" itself was born in those ages of darkness and superstition when Popish officials applied that holy act to church bells, candles, water, oil, crosses, pictures, bread, wine, and many other things; but that the "consecration" ever came from heaven, or was ever found in the Holy Scriptures of God, has never yet been proved, and that for the very conclusive reason that no man can prove an impossibility.

As to the *utility* of the practice, it would be a waste of words to dilate on a plea so useless; it never made a war

* Haydn's Book of Dates, pp. 68, 181, 266, 624.

† Henry's 'History of Britain,' vol. ii., p. 153.

holy, and never secured success; and, in the nature of things, it can never do the one or the other. It is a practical delusion from beginning to end, and remains a standing reproach to the name of Protestant England. The spread of pure Christianity will eventually destroy it, but popular admiration, imposed upon as it is by military displays and gewgaw exhibitions, may keep it alive for some time to come, but finally it will die away and be no more.

CHAPTER III.

AN EXAMINATION, ON CHRISTIAN PRINCIPLES, OF THE LAST CLAUSE IN THE 37TH ARTICLE OF THE CHURCH OF ENGLAND, WHICH ASSERTS IT LAWFUL FOR CHRISTIAN MEN TO WEAR WEAPONS, AND SERVE IN THE WARS. THE WHOLE CLAUSE READS THUS:—"*It is lawful for Christian men, at the commandment of the magistrate, to wear weapons, and serve in the wars.*"

"*We ought to obey God rather than men*" was the noble declaration of an inspired apostle, when "commanded" by the civil magistrate of that period "that they should not speak in the name of Jesus." The command was delivered with a stern authority that would have abashed an ordinary man, however righteous his cause might have been. But the case was intended to be an example and encouragement to all ages, and it was indispensable that the firmness should be equal to the necessity, and should teach the very important lesson that the Christian owes allegiance to a higher power than that of man.*

* Acts v. 29—40.

Two things connected with the apostolic case deserve close attention. *First*, that the civil magistrate may be in error, even when exercising his legitimate authority on his judgment seat; and, *second*, that under such circumstances the interests of truth require that the magistrate should not be obeyed.

Civil government is of divine appointment. Upon this question there ought not to be two opinions. "He beareth not the sword [of authority] in vain, for he is the minister of God." As these two points embrace the entire theory, and determine the limits, of civil government, their close and impartial examination is indispensable to a correct knowledge of the right of the Church of England to declare it "lawful" for Christian men, "at the commandment of the magistrate, to wear weapons and serve in the wars." It is a subject of solemn importance, and should be approached with all the gravity and care due to an enquiry that has to do with the lives of immortal men, and the solid welfare of society at large. And it is incumbent on all parties to remember that reverence for Holy Scripture is superior to all other considerations that can by any possibility bear upon the case; and that philosophy, expediency, and state policy, must alike bow to the divine authority that utters its eternal mandates with "Thus saith the Lord."

That supreme voice has spoken out from the invisible glory, and proclaimed the law—the profound, unalterable, and eternal law—to universal man, "THOU SHALT NOT KILL." Is it not enough that the incorruptible God, who "cannot lie, and will not repent," has thus declared and affirmed it before the universe, that MAN SHALL NOT KILL.

MAN? It is no ambiguous, uncertain utterance, but a divine prohibition, as extensive, and as binding, and as perpetual, as the kindred law, "Thou shalt not steal;" the one protecting the property, as the other protects the infinitely more valuable *life*, of man. The one guarding the honest gains, but the other performing the far higher office of protecting the *existence*, of the man. Does thislaw, any more than others that form parts of the same great moral code, require to be incessantly repeated in order to be understood and obeyed? Is it not plain, explicit, and beyond all doubt and cavil? Is it not the authoritative declaration of the Most High, that He reserves to himself the right and the power to take the life He gave? or, in other words, is it not the assertion of His own unimpeachable prerogative to "kill?" And while He reserves this right to himself, is it not self-evident that He withholds it from *all* His creatures, permitting none of them, whether rulers or the ruled, whether sovereigns or subjects, to invade His own supreme right, or to innovate upon His divine property?

To qualify such a law is virtually to destroy it, for being universal, as all *divine* laws must ever be, whensoever and by whomsoever it is bound about by limitations it ceases to be universal, and the moment it ceases to be universal *that* moment it ceases to be divine. It follows, therefore, beyond all controversy, that by what means soever this great law is suspended, or contravened, it is so far repealed, and for all its intended purposes it is rendered null and void. In such a condition it is no longer the law of the Eternal God, but is degraded to the low level of a human expedient, where obedience is no more than a partial virtue, and disobedience no longer a sin.

But by what right, or by whose authority, is the Church of England guilty of this very enormity,—this direct opposition to the law of Him who made heaven and earth? By what process of sound reasoning or legitimate argument can this right be proved? For, obviously, it is not enough for that church, or any other, merely to *assume* the lawfulness of the magisterial act to call out men to kill, when the law of the great God condemns killing as a sin, for sin is evermore "the transgression of the law."* Something more weighty and conclusive than official assumption, or mere Pagan custom, derived, in all probability, from the Trojan War, from a Homer, a Virgil, a Constantine, or a Charlemagne, is required, and ought to be supplied without the slightest delay, to show that the magistrate is empowered and authorised to suspend the law of the Ruler of the universe in favour of killing mankind in war. This law, let it ever be remembered, is the rule of duty, the basis of honour and virtue, and the pledge of safety to all that obey it. Perfect in all its requirements, because it is the law of God, it reigns supreme over all human law, and merits the homage of all mankind. To disobey it, whether by the individual man or the magistrate, is to challenge a punishment from which there can be no possible escape. It follows, therefore, that if the magistrate, on whatever plea, will persist in calling out men to kill their fellowmen, he must abide the consequences of his own disobedience; but it will be to his interest to bear in mind that, sooner or later, a retributive Providence will find ways and means to teach him the inevitable—the irreversible truth—that "all they

* 1 John iii. 4.

that take the sword shall perish with the sword;" and this solemn truth may be said to be written in letters of flame on the ruins of a Babylon, a Persia, a Greece, and a Rome, with numerous other once-flourishing nations upon earth. "God is not mocked," is a terrible warning to mankind at large; and when the magistrate "mocks" by disobedience to the divine law, his final fate will but confirm the fearful assurance that "Whatsoever a man soweth, that shall he also reap."*

This sacred right to dispose of human life has been reserved to the Most High from the earliest age of the human race. It was written on the existence, if not stamped on the brow, of a murderous Cain, whom heaven permitted no other man to punish or destroy; and it preserved the life of that murderer, "lest any finding him should kill him." It appeared in a new connection immediately after the flood, by making it a providential statute that whoso shed man's blood should in due time shed his own. The punishment of the murderer was thus committed to the government of the divine providence which thenceforth stood pledged to see that the guilty did not escape. When more distinct law became a necessity, in consequence of the increasing corruption of the race, then express legislation appeared in the Mosaic ritual, and surrounded human life with the minutest care and the most cautious instructions; but at the back of that imposing ceremonial, there stood the Supreme authority defining the limits of the magisterial office, and pointing out how and when and where he might touch the divine property in taking the life of man. It was not given to him to

* Galatians vi. 7 8.

issue a "commandment" to the tribes "to wear weapons and serve in the wars," without express direction from the unseen, yet ever-present, proprietor of human existence, who, by the Urim and the Thummim, ordered or forbade any war according to His own sovereign will. When He dictated a war, it then became the duty of the host to obey; but when He forbade it, or was silent, then the people did not dare leave their tents. The work of war was that of the Lord of Hosts, and not that of the civil magistrate in any sense whatever; and underlying the whole economy there existed an awful power that practically exclaimed, "The life of man is mine, and you shall not make war upon it, but as I command." This invisible presence issued the mysterious permission to slaughter the Canaanites and the neighbouring wicked nations; but with that punitive arrangement the Jewish magistrate, whether in the person of a Moses or a Joshua, had nothing whatever to do but to obey. The Almighty himself ordered the war, assigned its limits, and minutely described the objects which it was intended to accomplish; but the *right* so to act He reserved to himself. Consequently, there is no analogy whatever between the Jewish wars and the arrogant and persistent claim of the Church of England in its 37th Article; for God was ever present in the one instance; but will any bishop, or other official, venture the bold assertion that He is equally present in the other? The same strain of remark will also apply to the life and wars of David—"the man after God's own heart"—for in all the great transactions of his chequered career, he "enquired of the Lord" and obtained his warlike instructions direct from the Most High. But while this was done with both piety and prayer, and in all his warlike course, a special blessing rested upon him; yet, as if the Almighty One intended to show in that eminent patriarch His extreme aversion to war, and that He permitted it but for a period of darkness and ignorance, until "the fulness of time" should come, for the appearance of David's greater son, "the Prince of Peace,"—He prohibited that warlike ruler from building His temple, because he had been a man of blood and had made great wars. The prohibition was a memorable one, and should be carefully studied by every Christian. It ran in these words:—"Thou hast shed blood abundantly, and hast made great wars; thou shalt not build an house unto My name, because thou hast shed much blood upon the earth in my sight."* What is the profound moral taught by this remarkable case but the one that modern nations, though called *Christian*, are among the last to learn, namely, that the cause of God is not served by men of blood? The eminent psalmist, notwithstanding his devotion and pious zeal, might not touch God's sacred house because his fingers were defiled with blood; and what better fate can theirs be, who "consecrate" colours intended to do honour to deeds of blood, such as the Divine Being condemned in the person of David?

The right claimed by our Maker throughout all the ancient dispensations, to the sole disposal of human life, is perpetuated and strengthened by new sanctions in the Christian economy, and this of necessity arising out of the natural relations existing between the different administrations of the Most High. The moral government, of which

* 1 Chronicles xxii. 8.

the moral law is the authorised exposition, is the basis of them all, and must ever remain the same, world without end. Mere ceremonials, and ritual services of all kinds, which have but a remote, if any, connection with morals, can be superseded or annulled, according to the will of the Supreme Legislator. Being intended for temporary purposes, when their end is answered, they may be replaced by others, as the Divine Ruler may see fit. But not so with the moral law, which, from its evident nature and design, must be perpetual, and will ever remain the same: changing dispensations will pass away with the times to which they belonged; but "till heaven and earth pass, one jot or one tittle shall in no wise pass from the law, till all be fulfilled."*

From these premises it follows, as an inevitable consequence, that the reserved right of the Great Supreme to the sole disposal of human life is as prominent in the Gospel as it was in the original statute law, and that the prohibition, "Thou shalt not kill," is as binding on all men this day as it was in any former age. It is evident, therefore, that the 37th Article of the Church of England is not supported by Holy Scripture, and that the magistrate has no power whatever from God to "command" any class of men "to wear weapons and serve in the wars." It is an assumption without proof, and encourages a cruel practice, for which that church can plead no authority from the word of God, and it contradicts its own teaching, as given in Article 20, which expressly declares that the church may not "so expound one place of Scripture that it be repugnant to another."

* Matthew v. 18.

The genius and entire scope of Christianity are widely different from the prior economy of Moses, which, though divine, was both special and temporary:—special, as intended for special purposes among a small section of the human family; and temporary, as being but "a shadow of good things to come, and not the very image of the things" foreshadowed. But when the time had come for the manifestation of the substances, then the shadow withdrew, as being no longer required. And surely no sensible man will be so wanting to himself, and to the broad interests of Christian truth, as to affirm that the "shadow" was better than the substance; and that it would have been to the advantage of mankind at large had that "shadow" remained instead of the substance. But, believing that the substance is unspeakably more valuable than the shadow, it is both proper and natural to inquire what is that substance, and how far does it affect the power of the magistrate to command men to "serve in the wars;" or, in other words, "does the gospel of redeeming love warrant the magistrate, or any other official, to command and employ men to kill one another?"

It is most evident, beyond all contradiction, that the "substance" is the gospel of Jesus Christ, and that the Mosaic dispensation was the divinely appointed "shadow" of the greater glory that was to follow. Proofs of this could be easily supplied from the whole of that ancient ritual, were they necessary to the present argument; but it is enough to say that from the Jewish High Priest down through the numerous sacrifices, and the whole of the tabernacle service, the dispensation was one huge "shadow of good things to come;" but when "that which was perfect had come, then that which was in part was done away." The "shadow" then gave place to the substance, and departed to return no more. "If, then, that which was done away was glorious, much more that which remaineth is glorious;" yet it is of the first importance to remember that glorious as the dispensation of Moses undoubtedly was, in comparison with the all-surrounding heathenism of those dark ages, its glory was more than eclipsed, "by reason of the glory that excelleth."* With all that was sacred and sublime in that distinguished economy, it dwindles into a very "shadow" in the presence of the gospel of God's eternal love.†

Here, then, we are reduced to the necessity of considering the bearings of this noble Christianity on magisterial action, and to assert in the broadest and most emphatic manner that in many particulars what was proper under Moses would be improper under Christ, who is, confessedly, superior to Moses, as the master is evermore superior to the mere "servant." The one governed by rigid law, but the other by heavenly love; the one being the legal administrator dealt in punishments, but the other deals in pardon; the one was marked by severity, but the other by tender pity and compassion; the voice of the one was "Do this and live," but the voice of the other is, "Father, forgive them, for they know not what they do." Within the sanctions of the Mosaic economy, war, capital punishments, domestic slavery, and polygamy, all found an equal tolerance or an equal place; but when Jesus Christ came He swept them all away, and esta-

* 2 Corinthians iii. 10, 11. † See Appendix D.

blished in their stead the universal law of love.* This holy law, therefore, is the permanent rule for the government of mankind; and having for ever superseded the temporary provisions of the Mosaic code, it proclaims to the world this matchless truth, "Love worketh no ill to his neighbour, therefore love is the fulfilling of the law."†

It would be a perfect waste of words to refute the superficial plea that the civil magistrate is exempted from the operation of this law, since it is utterly impossible that any creature, in any capacity whatsoever, can be exempted from the divine law, *except by express legislation.* Under the dispensation of Moses, the magistrate, and the people generally, possessed this kind of exceptive legislation, as the foregoing remarks clearly show; but under the far more perfect rule of Christianity no such distinction is permitted, but alike to all, whether the magistrate or the private subject, it declares with the utmost impartiality the universal rule of action, in these distinct terms:—"If ye fulfil the royal law according to the scripture, Thou shalt love thy neighbour as thyself, ye do well: but if ye have respect to persons, ye commit sin, and are convinced of the law as transgressors. For whosoever shall keep the whole law, and yet offend in one point, he is guilty of all. *Yet if thou kill*, thou art become a transgressor of the law.‡

Consequently, the 37th Article of the Church of England is clearly anti-Christian, since it is evident that the magis-

* Deut. vii. 1, 2; Deut. xx. throughout; Lev. ix. 9, 10; Lev. xxiv. 16, 17; Exodus xxi. 1—6; Deut. xxi. 10—17.

† Romans xiii. 10.

‡ James ii. 8—11.

trate is nowhere authorised under the gospel to command Christian men "to wear weapons and serve in the wars." The act is an open violation of the purest law the universe has ever known, and when committed by the magistrate he abuses the authority with which he is invested; and in an office where he is solemnly bound to perform the part of a *Christian* ruler, there, by transgressing the law of love, he becomes, in his actions, *a heathen or a Jew*.

This painful conclusion could be made still more apparent from an examination of the special injunctions of the Holy Scriptures, such as the following, to which numerous additions might readily be made:—

"*Love your enemies, bless them that curse you, do good to them that hate you, and pray for them which despitefully use you, and persecute you.*"—Matt. v. 44.

"*Avenge not yourselves.—If thine enemy hunger, feed him; if he thirst, give him drink.—Recompense to no man evil for evil.—Overcome evil with good.*"—Romans xii. 19, 20, 21.

"*By this shall all men know that ye are my disciples, if ye have love one to another.*"—John xiii. 35.

"*Be ye all of one mind, having compassion one of another; love as brethren; be pitiful, be courteous, not rendering evil for evil, or railing for railing.*"—1 Peter iii. 8, 9.

"*Put up again thy sword into his place; for all they that take the sword shall perish with the sword.*"—Matt. xxvi. 52.

"*For the weapons of our warfare are not carnal, but mighty through God.*"—2 Cor. x. 4.

Is it for any such purposes as these that the magistrate commands "Christian men to wear weapons and serve in the wars?" Can he, with all his authority, "command" such men to be Christians upon the battle-field, and there to forgive and love the enemy,—to feed him and to give him drink? He knows well that in the fiendish strife of war, Christianity is totally surrendered, and that violence, murder, and death are systematically permitted to take its place. It comes, therefore, to this one point, that no magistrate upon earth has authority from God to command men to "serve in the wars," those wars being so utterly opposed to the spirit, the practice, and merciful design of the Christian faith. The act is one of open defiance of the Saviour, and as far as it may, it converts the gospel of His love into a source of sorrow to the whole world.

It is impossible to deplore too deeply this system of contradictions, and these acts of the magistrate, that do so much to encourage and perpetuate the wickedness of war among mankind. Acts such as these keep alive the war spirit throughout christendom to an appalling extent, the magistrate in one nation vieing with the magistrate of another nation in a despicable rivalry to raise the largest number of fighting men, to appear on some future occasion in a deadly strife, which none of them study to avoid. Practically, they invite the strife by the preparations they make to meet it; for having "commanded" the men "to wear weapons and serve in the wars," it is but taking another step in the same direction to provoke wars in which to exhibit their untried prowess. The real danger lies in arming the magistrate with the tremendous power of creating the explosive material, which at any unexpected moment may scatter death among innocent thousands of mankind. But this destructive power a loving Christianity never conferred upon the magistrate, and that for the profound reason that it never can, but as it denies itself.

It is equally to be deplored that this most unauthorised claim on behalf of the magistrate does its full part to postpone, indefinitely, that glorious period of the future, set before us all with so much of poetic beauty and brilliance in the various pages of holy writ. In that day of the Redeemer's glory there shall be "abundance of peace so long as the moon endureth;" then "the wolf also shall dwell with the lamb; and the leopard shall lie down with the kid; and the calf and the young lion and the fatling together; and a little child shall lead them. . . . They shall not hurt nor destroy; for the earth shall be full of the knowledge of the Lord, as the waters cover the sea." "They shall beat their swords into ploughshares, and their spears into pruning-hooks; nation shall not lift up sword against nation, neither shall they learn war any more."* In that glowing era of the world's deliverance from the soldier and the sword, no magistrate will be daring enough to "command" men "to wear weapons and serve in the wars." His office then will be of a far nobler character than the one with which a feeble and diluted Christianity now invests him; and, instead of the language of a vulgar heroism, which at present he too frequently employs, his voice will be heard in the chorus of an emancipated universe, exclaiming, "*Blessed are the peacemakers, for they shall be called the children of God.*"† Let men designate that "golden age" by the name of the *Millennium*, if that too little understood term best expresses its character and greatness; but let them not fall into the serious error of supposing that the Millennium will banish

* Isaiah ii. 4, and Isaiah xi. 6—9.

† Matthew v. 9.

war, and so be content to sit still, waiting with idle expectancy for that period to do the mighty work, which they are *solemnly bound to do for themselves.* This has proved a fatal misconception on the part of the Christian world for ages, and has led to a guilty indolence, which perpetuates the curse of war throughout the whole earth. The Millennium is not a *cause*, but an *effect* ; and the true teaching of Holy Scripture is not that the Millennium will abolish war, but that "THE ABOLITION OF WAR WILL BRING THE MILLENNIUM!"

And in this honourable work of preparing for that blessed day, where is there, or where can there be, a more powerful body of workers than the clergy of the Church of England? Other sections of the universal church have their eminent men,—men devoted, learned, and earnest, above most others about them; but for ready unity of action, and the *possible* concentration of effort for any given work of the age, there is no one ecclesiastical body in christendom to compare with the clergy of that church. Having influence with the people, and in the Senate, superior to that of any other class of ministers of religion, what could they not do for the world at large, and for Great Britain in particular, were they uniformly men of peace according to the Holy Scriptures? What war system on earth could long stand before them? The public opinion of the nations would very soon be in their hands, to mould, fashion, and shape it into conformity with the Word of God. But, unfortunately, the 37th Article of their own church, warps their opinions and fetters their action in any effort on behalf of universal peace. That unscriptural article imposes on their own ministerial consciences; and then, often without knowing it, they in turn impose on the people. Would to heaven they would be bold and brave enough to revoke that pernicious article! Would that they were resolved, once for all, to place our beloved country at the head of the world in "learning war no more." This high, imperishable honour, above all that Great Britain has ever known, is even yet within their grasp. Let but my lord of Canterbury openly proclaim that our country, having obtained as much of glory as bloodshed and battle-fields are likely to confer, will henceforth seek for further honour in the field of sacred peace *alone;* let him so lead on his noble army of ministerial brethren to a new consecration to the work of their great Master, "The Prince of Peace," and ages and generations to come will have reason to bless God for having bestowed on the human race,

THE PROTESTANT CHURCH OF ENGLAND!

APPENDIX A.

(*Page* 11.)

Specimen of Consecration by Archbishop Laud.

[The bishop came, attended with several of the high commission and some civilians. At his approach to the west door of the church, which was shut and guarded by halberdiers, some that were appointed for that purpose, cried, with a loud voice, *Open, open, ye everlasting doors, that the King of glory may come in!* Presently, the doors were opened, and the bishop, with some doctors and principal men, entered. As soon as they were within the place, his lordship fell down upon his knees, and with eyes lifted up, and his arms spread abroad, said, *This place is holy—the ground is holy: in the name of the Father, Son, and Holy Ghost, I pronounce it holy.* Then, walking up the middle aisle, towards the chancel, he took up some of the dust, and threw it into the air several times. When he approached near the rail of the communion table, he bowed towards it five or six times, and returning, went round the church, with his attendants, in procession, saying, first the hundredth, and then the nineteenth psalm, as prescribed in the Roman pontifical. He then read several collects, in one of which he prays God *to accept of that beautiful building*, and concludes thus:—"*We consecrate this church, and separate it unto Thee as holy ground, not to be profaned any more to common use.*" In another he prays "*That all who should hereafter be buried within the circuit of this holy and sacred place, may rest in their sepulchres in peace till Christ's coming to judgment, and may then rise to eternal life and happiness.*"

The bishop then, sitting under a cloth of state, in the aisle of the chancel, near the communion table, proceeded with a "commination" of about twenty *curses* on all who should profane that sacred place; and these were succeeded by a like number of blessings on such as gave anything towards its erection. Then came the sermon, then the sacrament, which he consecrated and administered thus:—"As he approached the altar, he made five or six low bows, and coming up to the side of it, where the bread and wine were covered, he bowed *seven* times. Then, after other such genuflexions, he first received the *consecrated* elements, then he gave them to the principal men in their surplices, hoods, and tippets; and, after many prayers being offered, the consecration ended."—*Slightly abridged from Towgood,* '*On Dissent,*' pp. 261—3.]

Towgood appears to have taken the above from Prynne's complete History, p. 114. It may also be seen in Rushworth's 'Collections,' vol. i., p. 77; as given by Neal in his '*History of the Puritans.*' vol. i., pp. 540—2.

APPENDIX B.

(Page 27.)

The "Burials" Question.

It is not a matter "of good repute" for the clergy, when the *politician* excels them in charity and forbearance towards those Christians who differ from themselves. Of all men in the world ministers of religion should be the most humane and tender-hearted; but it often happens to be the reverse, as the following case will show:—Mr. C. E. Lewis, M.P. for Londonderry, had been censured by some of his narrow-minded constituents for voting in favour of the "Burials' Bill;" and, in reply to their censures, he addressed them in these manly terms:—"My conduct in this matter is based solely upon a desire not only to do justice to Dissenters, but prevent injury to the Church of England. Although it is no business of mine, I venture to think that you will not advance your cause by such an intolerable circular. Several Conservative members told me last session that they never would again vote against the bill, and if they are left to the exercise of conscientious convictions there will be a majority for the bill. I want to maintain the Church of England, and not to destroy it. The bigotry and intolerance, however, of such men as raise the question of the title of 'reverend' do more to destroy it than ten campaigns of the Liberation Society."

The politician is right, for "bigotry and intolerance" never yet served any good cause, and never will. But the most painful part of the matter is, that the clergy can never injure themselves without injuring the religion whose interests are entrusted to their care. They wound their divine Christianity in the house of its own friends.

It is but fair, however, to state that an influential section of the clergy are men of more generous sentiments, as the following memorial will show:—"We, the undersigned clergymen of the Church of England, desire to urge respectfully upon her Majesty's Government that it would be for the advantage of the Church that the burials' controversy should be settled without further delay by some reasonable concession to the feelings of Nonconformists. And we suggest that in any legislative measure to be introduced for this purpose, permission should be given to a recognised minister or representative of any religious body to perform in the churchyard a funeral service consisting only of passages of Holy Scripture, prayers, and hymns; and that the obligations of the clergy in respect of the use of the burial service should be modified at the same time in such manner as may be deemed expedient."

This memorial was signed by the deans of Chester, Durham, Canterbury, and Westminster, and by a very considerable number of clergymen in various parts of the kingdom. Such men do honour to their name.

The following, which took place during the present year, 1876, exhibits a deplorable want of charity and kind-heartedness to the bereaved and sorrowing relatives:—"At Nether Heyford, Northamptonshire, an infant lately died, and the vicar was applied to to name the hour (on the 18th inst.) for its burial. Finding that the child had not been baptized, he fixed eight o'clock at night, and when reminded that that was unreasonably late, he replied, 'I will tell the sexton to have the grave ready punctually at eight, but it shan't be before.' The Rev. W. H. Payne, Baptist minister, thereupon offered to conduct a service in his chapel, and on a dark, wet night, by the aid of lanterns, the chapel was reached, and the service took place. Just outside the churchyard a prayer was offered, and amid profound silence the body was lowered into the grave."

APPENDIX C.

(*Page* 34.)

War Prayers.

In the *Annual Register* for 1788, page 120, the Rev. Dr. T. Nash contributes a paper from "the Society of Antiquaries of London," which contains the following prayer by the unfortunate Katherine Parr, the sixth and last wife of that versatile monarch, Henry VIII., King of England. If it exhibits less of scholarship, it is also much less *heathenish* than that of Archdeacon Wilberforce, and to some extent it breathes the true spirit of humanity and Christianity. It was written during the French war and the King's expedition into France, and seems preferable to the prayer directed by the liturgy to be used in time of war. It runs thus:—"Our cause being just, and being enforced to enter into war and battle, we most humbly beseech thee, O Lord God of Hosts, so to turn the hearts of our enemies to the desire of peace, that no Christian blood be spilt; or else, grant, O Lord, that with small effusion of blood, and to the little hurt of innocents, we may, to thy glory, obtain victory, and that, the wars being soon ended, we may all with one heart and mind, knit together in concord and unity, laud and praise thee, O Lord." This, to my ears, says Dr. Nash, sounds better than, "abate their pride, assuage their malice, and confound their devices."

APPENDIX D.

(*Page* 50.)

The earned Hugo Grotius puts this great truth in a very homely way in the following words:—"Neither will it follow, that because the law given by Moses was good, therefore a better could not be given. Parents are wont to lisp with their children, to wink at the faults of their age, to tempt them to learn with a cake; but as they grow up, their speech is corrected, the precepts of virtue instilled into them, and they are shown the beauty of virtue, and what are its rewards. . . . . And in that state, it was reasonable some things should be overlooked, which were then to be reduced to a more perfect rule, when God by a greater power of his Spirit was to gather to himself a new people out of all nations."—*Vide* "*Grotius on the Truth of Religion*," book 5, sec. 6.

The Modern Druid.

(*Pages* 33, 34.)

The following poem was written at Stonehenge, on Salisbury Plain, a few days after the consecration of colours and the prayer of Archdeacon Wilberforce, as given at pages 33 and 34. The allusions are exclusively to the exhibition of that ecclesiastic when engaged in the service of the God of War:—

"In days of yore the Druid sage
Assembled here his clan,
And from the dark and mystic page
Spoke war and woe to man;

Or from within this sacred spot,
With horrid Moloch rites,
Gave forth the black and dreadful lot
To rule their savage fights.

He told of war and vengeful dire,
To every conquer'd foe;
He doom'd each captive wretch to fire,
And bade the embers glow.

But NOW, no more the frantic dance,
Nor cruel Moloch glare;
No warrior comes to break his lance,
No Druid to his prayer.

No more the human victim bleeds
On altar built of earth;
No more are done the deadly deeds
That raised a Druid's mirth.

For other men spread o'er the land,
With nobler, gentler laws;
No Druid priest now leads his band
To desolating wars.

Save, where on yonder chosen plain
Gay banners float around,
And warlike hosts obey the strain
Of music's martial sound.

There stands the priest in solemn guise,
(No Druid's name he bears),
And turns to heaven his lifted eyes,
And pours to Heaven his prayers.

'Oh! God of mercy, God of love,
To whom we owe our breath,
Pour down thy grace from Heav'n above,
And bless the work of death.

'Go forth, O God, with these to war,
In battle give them skill,
Write in their hearts the martial law,
And teach them how to kill.'

Oh, sacred pile! this solemn prayer
Inspires a solemn dread;
For all its earnest cries declare
'THE DRUID IS NOT DEAD.'"

T. P. NEWMAN, PRINTER, 32, BOTOLPH LANE, EASTCHEAP, E.C.